Anonymous

Observations on the Principles and Tendency of the East India Bills

Proposed by the Right Honourable Charles James Fox, and the Right Honourable William Pitt, with short sketches of their political characters

Anonymous

Observations on the Principles and Tendency of the East India Bills
Proposed by the Right Honourable Charles James Fox, and the Right Honourable William Pitt, with short sketches of their political characters

ISBN/EAN: 9783337012588

Printed in Europe, USA, Canada, Australia, Japan

Cover: Foto ©Suzi / pixelio.de

More available books at **www.hansebooks.com**

OBSERVATIONS

ON THE

PRINCIPLES AND TENDENCY

OF THE

EAST INDIA BILLS

PROPOSED BY

The Right Honourable CHARLES JAMES FOX,

AND

The Right Honourable WILLIAM PITT,

WITH

Short Sketches of their Political Characters.

Simul fuis virtutibtus, fimul vitiis aliorum in ipfam gloriam praceps agebatur. TACIT. DE VIT. AGRICOLÆ.

LONDON:

Printed for J. STOCKDALE, oppofite Buriington-Houfe, Piccadilly. 1784.

PRICE ONE SHILLING AND SIX.PENCE.

OBSERVATIONS,

&c. &c. &c.

THOUGH I am not a Member of
Parliament, yet as an Englifhman,
enjoying the bleffings of the Conftitution,
I am effentially interefted in every meafure
which can either directly, or collaterally af-
fect its ftability, injure its perfection, or
contaminate its ‑purity ; uninfluenced by
prejudice to party, or partiality to men,
my *attention* has been ferioufly turned to
the confideration of the different means,
which have been propofed for the attainment of that univerfally-acknowledged neceffary object, *A better government and ma-*

nagement

nagement of our concerns in the East-Indies.
I shall make no apology for offering to the
public the sentiments and opinion of an
undistinguished individual of the nation,
upon a subject which has been so ably dif-
cussed, and so long contested by the greatest
men, and most distinguished political characters of this political country. The fo-
phistry of particular systems, and the pro-
fessed predeterminations of party combina-
tion, have cramped the abilities, disordered
the judgment, and lessened the weight of
the eminent persons who have exerted them-
selves on either side of the question. As an
unprejudiced man, concerned only for the
safety and existence of a Constitution, from
whose prosperity I derive happiness, and in
whose destruction my dearest interests must
be involved; I feel it my duty to submit the
result of my observation and reflections to
the consideration and judgment of my fel-
low subjects.

The state of the India Company, from
great acquisition of property, within a short
period, has involved the interests of the
State

State fo much with thofe of the Company, as to make the politics and refources of the one in a great meafure dependent upon the adminiftration of the other : the im- menfe field opened for the operations of war and revenue in the Eaft, have prefented temptations to the ambition and avarice of the Company's chief fervants abroad, too great (in the words of Lord Clive) for flefh and blood to refift; fcenes of devaflation and extortion, equal to thofe of a Roman Pro-Conful, in the moft depraved periods of that republic, have been for a feries of years exhibited in that country by the fervants of the Company ; who, with very few, and even thofe qualified exceptions, have been folely intent upon the gratification of their paffions, and the accumulation of wealth, whilft the interefts of the Company, and the Public, have been neglected, or facrificed in the purfuit of thofe objects, at the fame time that the character of the nation has been difgraced, and its name rendered odious by the means employed to attain them.—The commercial intereft of the Company lan- guifhing ; its capital depreciated ; and its
adminiftration

adminiftration become a fcene of jobbing, and intrigue, inftead of trade and induftry; were circumftances which early alarmed the Public; excited the atttention of the Legiflature, and called for its interference. In 1783 an act was paffed, regulating the adminiftration of the Company's affairs in India, and by laws appointing Perfons for that purpofe, with powers defined, and entrufted to them by the Legiflature; thefe regulations, however falutary they appeared in theory, were found ineffectual in practice; various circumftances, which it is not neceffary to particularize, added to the great temptations which perfons acting under it, had to deviate from its reftrictions; as well as the very complicated fcene of politics, which, in fome inftances, might make difcretionary exertions juftifiable, or even neceffary, have proved *that* arrangement at fo remote a diftance ineffectual: the preffure of temporary diftrefs from the events, difficulties, and burthens of war, added to the enormity of accumulated and growing abufes, called for a great and effectual interpofition of legiflative authority and

and wifdom. I fhall now examine the prin-
cipal claufes of the two Eaft-India Bills,
which have been prefented to the Houfe of
Commons, for the purpofe of remedying
thefe evils, and which have been feverally
rejected by different branches of the Legiflature ; I fhall confider the principles and
tendency of each, and endeavour from thence
to deduce the characters, tenets, and pur-
fuits of the two great political characters who
framed and introduced the different Bills : I
will firft begin with that which was firft
propofed.

The preamble of the Bill ftates, that
" Whereas diforders of an alarming nature
" and magnitude have prevailed, and do
" ftill continue and increafe, in the ma-
" nagement of the territorial poffeffions,
" the revenues, and the commerce of this
" kingdom in the Eaft-Indies; by means
" whereof the profperity of the natives
" hath been greatly diminifhed, and the
" valuable interefts of this nation in the
" faid territorial poffeffions, revenues, and
" commerce, have been materially impaired,
" and would probably fall into utter ruin
if

" if an immediate and fitting remedy were
" not provided; be it therefore enact-
" ed, &c."

The firſt meaſure propoſed in the Bill, as
a preliminary to the intended remedies, to
be applied to the evils enumerated in the
preamble, is a total deprivation of the
powers now veſted in the body of Proprietors, and in twenty-four Directors, choſen
by them for the management of their affairs; to transfer the ſame powers, or in
the words of the act, " all and ſingular,
" the powers and authorities which have
" been *at any time* heretofore veſted in, or
" lawfully exerciſed by, the ſaid Court of
" Directors, *hereby diſcontinued*, or Pro-
" prietors, or by the General Court of Pro-
" prietors," to *ſeven* Directors, who were
not to be choſen by the Proprietors, for
whoſe intereſt they were to be ſuppoſed to
act; the Bill, however, declared, that theſe
powers were to be ſubject to ſuch reſtrictions and limitations as by this act ſhould
be provided or directed. What were the
reſtrictions or *limitations* which this act *did*
provide?

provide ? I have attentively fought for them, and can find nothing but *extenfion* of power and *amplification* of patronage, wherever the regulations of this Bill deviate from the powers and authorities hitherto vefted in the General Court of Proprietors, and Court of Directors.

The Proprietors have now authority to chufe and appoint twenty-four Directors for the management of their political and commercial concerns, who are to continue in their office for four years, with a fuccefsive change of fix who every year go out of the Direction by feniority, and are fucceeded by fix new Directors, chofen by a General Court of Proprietors. The Bill propofed by Mr. Fox, was to have appointed nine affiftant Directors " for the *fole* purpofe " of ordering and managing the *commerce* of " the faid Company," allowing, however, the Proprietors of India ftock, to elect a fuccefsfor to any vacancy which might happen by death, removal, or otherwife, but giving at the fame time, an unlimited and uncontrouled power to the *feven* Directors,

B   of

of removing *ad libitum* any one or more of
the affiftant Directors, acting under them,
for the regulation of the *commercial* interefts of the Company : by this regulation,
the Proprietors of India Stock would have
been deprived of that privilege which every
Englifhman has a right to poffefs, of in-
trufting the *management* of his *private
property* to thofe, whofe knowledge, abilities, or integrity, he has experienced,
or can confide in ; for in this cafe,
the management of the greateft_ collective commercial property in Europe,
would have been vefted, in the firft
inftance, in the hands of men, not
anfwerable to the owners of that property
for their conduct, not chofen by them, not
even offered to their approbation, or fubject
to their negative ; and leaft the fhadow of
their departed rights of election, (which
the appointment to any vacancy which
might happen amongft the original nine
Directors gave them,) fhould bear any appearance of freedom, or confer any power
to elude the jealous grafp of minifterial influence, by the poffible introduction of
                                    any

any independant affiftant Directors; the
ancient eftablifhed mode of election by
ballot, was to have been abrogated, and a
book opened, in which a Proprietor with
any profpect, or hope of employment for
himfelf or any of his connections, muft be
rafh and inconfiderate indeed, to venture to
record his refractorinefs by figning his
name, as voting for a candidate obnoxi-
ous to, or *not recommended* by the Minifter; yet even the exertion of this right,
were it more fubftantial, would have placed
any profpect of poffible advantage to the
interefts of the Proprietors, at a very great
diftance—for the death, or removal of *five*
Directors at leaft muft happen, before they
could have even a *fuppofed* confidence in, or
probable expectation of any regard to their
interefts, from thofe affiftant Directors;
but to what muft that confidence and thofe
expectations be reduced, when thefe even-
tual objects of their choice, thefe men of
their controuled election, would have been
liable " to be difmiffed, for the difobe-
" dience of any order or orders they might
" receive," from a Court of Directors,

who,

who, refpectable as they may be, for their
private integrity and abilities, were, to fay
the leaft of them, ignorant of commerce,
and unacquainted with the true interefts of
the India Proprietors, either in Europe or
in India; though it muft be confeffed, they
were admirably chofen, for the purpofe of
vefting the whole of the enormous patronage of that country in the hands of the
Coalition which was to create them, as the
names of the moft powerful connections,
and thofe of the neareft relations and moft
devoted adherents of the coalefcing Parties
compofed the Lift.

The dominion of the Court of Directors
propofed by this Bill, was not, however,
to have been confined to the fpecious power
of difmiffing the Members of a fubordi-
nate Board acting immediately under them;
It was further to be enacted, " that the
" Directors, or the major part of them,
" fhould have full power and authority to
" remove, difplace, fufpend, *appoint*, con-
" firm, or *reftore* all and every perfon from
" or to any office, ftation, or capacity what-
" foever,

" foever, civil or military, in the fervice of
" the faid United Company, or within the
" limits of the faid United Company's
" Charters, or any of them, or any way
" concerned in the management of their
" affairs within this Kingdom or in India,
", whether any fuch perfon or perfons fhall
" have been nominated or appointed, in
" and by any Act, or any Acts of Parlia-
" ment, or howfoever nominated or ap-
" pointed." Here the Bill appears in its
true colours, points to its true objects,
and lays open its only effectual tendency:
Patronage; immediate, ample, uncondi-
tional, unbounded Patronage! No fpecious
precaution of reafons to be inferted in the
minutes of their proceedings, is here provided; all appointments by Act of Parliament or otherwife, whether civil or military, from a Governor-general to a Writer,
from a Commander in Chief to a Cadet,
were to be fubject to their power of immediate removal, without any motive but their
intereft or inclination; without any controul
but their moderation and confciences;
what could have refifted the powerful difpofal of fuch an immenfe Patronage of em-
ployments

ployments and places! neverthelefs, more was thought neceffary " to make affurance double fure."

One fhould have imagined that the ex-clufive difpofal of Governments, military commands, commiffariats, contracts, fhip-ping, with the innumerable branches which fpread out from thofe great Stems of influ-ence and patronage, would have been fuffi-cient to fatisfy rapacious and ambitious men of any precedented inordinancy; but not fatisfied with depriving the Proprietors of Eaft India Stock of the right they enjoy by the conftitution of the country, and the contract of their Charter, to choofe thofe, to whom they would delegate the *manage-ment* of their commercial concerns, and to whom they would confide places of the higheft truft, and of the moft effential con-fequence to their property; by this Bill, that very property was to have been wref-ted out of their hands, their fhips, books, warehoufes, merchandife, was to be feized upon, and committed to the uncontrouled management of men, who had no intereft in their concerns, no knowledge of their affairs

affairs, and no refponfibility to them, or indeed to any body: the Directors were, it is true, to offer their books, for the infpection of the Proprietors every fix months; but to what purpofe could be this exhibition of accounts, before perfons, to whom they were not amenable, whofe difapprobation would be as impotent as their applaufe would be futile; for the Directors could only have been removed before the end of their commiffion, by an addrefs from a Parliament to whom they would have had the power of diftributing two millions per annum ! Such a provifion for the removal of the Directors was an infult on the defigned impotency of the Eaft India Company: The premature influence of fuch a Bill, is the beft warning of its dangerous tendency, what is to be expected from the experienced enjoyments of its corrupting fweets, when the bare hopes of its untafted benefits could carry it through one branch of the legiflature !

When I fee charters violated; a Power exercifed over the perfons and interefts of thofe who did not delegate it; and the

property

property feized which has not been forfeited; I fhudder at the powers which I have hitherto revered; and whilft I rejoice at the timely and glorious interpofition of one branch of the Legiflature, which has faved us from the precipice, I cannot help looking with horror into the abyfs of wretchednefs and flavery to which we fhall fall, if ever the omnipotence of the conftitution fhould be ftretched to the verge of its power, and fink into tyranny.

Had this Bill paffed into a law, the Conftitution would have been deftroyed by the rafhnefs of the Legiflature; a rew executive power raifed above the controul of the Crown, fixed by the Parliament to a period beyond its own exiftence; armed with an independence of the prerogative of difmiffion, which the Parliament itfelf does not poffefs; and invefted with the boundlefs patronage and meafurelefs riches of the Eaft, would have ftarted up at once too formidable for fufferance, and too powerful for refiftance; a conteft would have immediately taken place between the old conftitutional executive power of the Crown, and this new monfter

monfter of executive ariftocracy: the
Crown, whofe fplendour by exciting jea-
loufy takes from its power, would probably have fallen the victim of the more vigorous though lefs glaring influence of the
rich and powerful ariftocracy it oppofed (if
the inftruments of one great conftituent and
directing man deferve that name;) but which-
foever gained the afcendancy the victory
muft have been deftructive to the Conftitution, and calamitous to the Nation; for my
own part I cannot hefitate to decide, and do
not fcruple to declare, that of the two
dreadful calamities, one of which muft have
enfued, I fhould prefer flavifh uncertainty
under an unlimited monarchy, to the fel-
fifh tyranny and rapacity exerted by a powerful ariftocracy; yet fubjection to the latter
would probably have been the fate of this
country, had Mr. Fox's Eaft India Bill paffed into a law, and his commiffioners ob-
tained their affured exiftence to a period
beyond that at which this Parliament muft
terminate. The riches of the Eaft, and the
influence of its patronage (the *whole* of which,
as I have before ftated, this Bill would have
given the Directors a power of vacating and

C   conferring

conferring at their pleafure,) muſt have en-
fured fuch a Parliament, after the general
election, as would have acted in whatever
manner the framer of this Bill fhould pleafe
to direct ; implicitly feconding his views,
adopting his meafures, and executing his
orders : The outward form of the old con-
ſtitution would have fcreened the encroachments of his power, till he had extended
it to fuch a degree of excefs and ftrength,
that he could, as it fuited his intereft, inclination, or ambition, either continue to exhi-
bit, or finally crufh the empty fhell of the
old form of Government.

It has been urged that the independence
of the feven Directors is not new to the Con-
ſtitution, and the fituation of the twelve
Judges has been adduced as a proof of
the aſſertion ; but a very few words
will be fufficient to point out the different
nature and tendency of a judicial, or an
executive authority independent of the
Crown. The Judges are bound to adhere in
their decifions to the common or ftatute laws
of the kingdom, which decifions are upon
proof of error liable to be reverfed by an
appeal

appeal to one of the branches of the Legiflature; but the feven Directors propofed by Mr. Fox's Eaft India Bill, unguided by laws, uncontrouled by appeals, were to have made the regulations by which they fhould act, " and bid their will avouch it;" they were not conftituted for the decifion, but for the affumption of property; they were not difinterefiedly to determine between thofe who applied to them for judgment, but to govern thofe who protefted againft their exiftence; they were not (like the Judges) to decide points to which the long and abftrufe ftudy of a learned profeffion was exclufively competent, and in which their eminence made them peculiarly excellent; they were to undertake the exclufive management of commercial concerns, in which they had no experience; and the unlimited government of an extenfive country, of which they had no knowledge; they were to unite a power of territory, an influence of patronage, and weight of wealth within themfelves, which could only be fafe to the country and conftitution, from the great numbers and divided interefts of

the

the Eaft-India Proprietors; in fhort, the parallel of the judges and of the propofed Eaft-India Directors, reduces itfelf to this conclufion, that the independence of the firft is neceffary to the fecurity of individuals and their property; the independence of the laft muft have been fubverfive of the rights, and deftructive to the liberties of the whole people. Having confidered the mifchiefs which would have arifen from this Bill to the conftitution at *Home*, I will proceed to examine how far its operation would have tended to remove or correct the evils which exift in the government of our territorial poffeffions in *India*.

To remedy the complaint which has been made, that the great property of the delinquent fervants of the Company in India, gave them too much weight and influence in the General Courts, by whom they were to be judged, this Bill was to have vefted the whole power of taking cognizance of crimes, and judging culprits in the new Court of Directors, who were to begin their examination, " twenty days " after

" after the receipt of any accufation or of-
" ficial account of difputes between the
" Governors and their refpective Councils,
" or between the government of one fet-
" tlement and the government of another
" fettlement, &c " and were to come to a
definitive decifion within three months, or
give their reafons for *not* having done fo; it
further provided, that no perfon accufed of
a crime in India, fhould be continued in a
place of power or truft, unlefs the Court of
Directors find fuch charge to be groundlefs,
or *not of fufficient importance to exclude the
faid perfon from the faid office.* To perfons
determined to do juftice, " for truth's fake,
and their confcience," no regulations are
neceffary; to men aiming at power, grafping
at influence, and greedy of patronage, thefe
regulations would be peculiarly favourable:
I do not mean to caft any imputation upon
the particular men who were propofed for
the offices of Directors or Commiffioners,
many of them are of the moft refpectable
characters, but fuch is the general depravity
of human nature, that mifconduct, ambition and venality, muft be provided againft
in

in all human regulations of policy and power; and whilst we are endeavouring to can-
cel and dispel the existing evils in India, we
must not hazard the growth of greater in-
conveniencies at home: if we should for a
moment suppose the new Court of Directors,
surrounded with needy, clamorous, and rapacious dependants, should we suppose them
eager to exert their powers, and provide for
their croud of followers and their numerous
families; could any thing be more amply
adapted to their purposes, than the provi-
sions I have already cited from the Bill? In
twenty days after the receipt of any accusa-
tion or complaint they are to begin examination, and to proceed to *definitive* judgment before the end of three months, or
give their reasons for *not* having done so—
no reason is required for their *having* come
to any decision they please; it is therefore at
their option to give a *definitive* judgment
upon partial accusations, supported by
ex parte evidence, which published, will give
a specious reason for the recall of any official
person, from the highest to the lowest, in
India; and this judgment, except on extra-
ordinary

ordinary occasions, is to be given within three months, a space of time which various accidents may make the difference of passage between two ships, quitting India nearly at the same time, the one bringing the refutation, the other the charges : Supposing all the present great offices in India so vacated, and filled by the needy dependents I have hypothetically described, the question will naturally be asked, Whether these officers may not be removed as their predecessors were ? No. For if one can suppose partiality or favour to exist in the breasts of the seven Directors, or any four of them, any charge may " appear to them *not of sufficient importance* to exclude the said person from the said office ;" and if it could be supposed that an immense acquisition of wealth by the persons nearly connected with, or formerly dependent upon them, would have equal influence on these seven Directors, as the same power of wealth acquired by men who from inferior offices, in the Company's service, had upon the whole collective body of Proprietors, what a terrible scene of

increased

increafed peculation, what an unprece-
dented (even in thofe countries) excefs of
fcreened villainy, and fearlefs oppreffion,
might we look forward to, from a new
fwarm of hungry adventurers, fent to fucceed the prefent leeches, who nearly filled,
fuck flowly, and without exertion, from
that long lacerated and bleeding country!
yet the worft that imagination can frame,
would, (under Directors or Commiffioners,
corruptible in themfelves, or furrounded and
influenced by needy dependants have been the
probable confequences) of the unbounded
difcretion of hafty condemnation, or the
arbitrary appreciation of the importance and
nature of fpecified and fubftantiated crimes,
which would have been delegated to them;
fuch a Bill appointing Commiffioners with
the ordinary frailties of human nature, ought
properly to be entitled, *An Act for the greater
oppreffion of the Natives of India, and for
the more fpeedy diffolution of our commercial
concerns and territorial poffeffions in that
country.*

I will

I will now proceed to the confideration of the Bill for the better government and management of the affairs of the Eaft-India Company, which was propofed by Mr. Pitt, and thrown out by the Houfe of Commons, on the queftion for the fecond reading of it, by a majority of eight votes, on Friday the 23d of January. Had the majority been more confiderable, I fhould with greater diffidence and hefitation have expreffed my opinion of this Bill, but with fo nearly one half of the Houfe of Commons in favour of an Act, which would have affumed no patronage, and confequently held forth no hopes of perfonal advantage, or emolument to thofe who fhould fupport it, I feel no fcruple to declare, that I think it was a Bill, which, with the grace of moderation, appeared to poffefs the excellence of efficacy; it gave interference, without influence, to the Crown, and vefted in the Government of this country the power of correction, and controul in India, unbiaffed by motives of intereft, or the exertion of patronage; it was a brilliant inftance of the unequalled abi-

D   lities,

lities, and characteriſtic diſintereſtedneſs
and moderation of the Right Honourable
framer of the Bill ; to give the power of
removal from offices without the privilege
of appointing officers ; to leave the choice
of able and experienced men to thoſe who
know the nature of the buſineſs to be un-
dertaken, and the talents and knowledge of
thoſe appointed to execute it, and to veſt
the power of recall in the Government,
who were competent to judge of the conduct of thoſe officers, and of the conſe-
quences likely to reſult from it to the be-
nefit, or detriment of the nation at large.——
But the Bill deſerves minute inveſtigation,
and will, I believe, appear in the moſt favourable light, from being ſubjected to the
moſt accurate examination. The firſt eſ-
ſential object of attention in the tranſactions
and regulations of the Eaſt-India Company,
is the effect they will have on the revenue
of this nation, and the political concerns of
this country in Europe ; a board of Commiſſioners was therefore propoſed in this
Bill, who ſhould " be fully authorized and
" impowered, from time to time, to check,
" ſuperintend,

" fuperintend, and controul all Acts, opera-
" tions, and concerns, which in any wife
" relate to the *civil* or *military* GOVERN-
" MENT, or *revenues* of the territories and
" poffeffions of the faid United Company,
" in the Eaft-Indies;"—here we fee the
real objects feized upon, which call for the
interpofition of Goverment, the *territorial*
concerns, the civil and military tranfactions,
and the revenue arrangements of the Company, not the private property and commercial regulations of the mere mercantile
Members of this great chartered body. No
mifmanagement of commerce could be of
fo dangerous a tendency, as to require fuch
violent meafures, as an arbitrary affumption
of the property of the Merchants—*Quid*
meruere .... *animal fine fraude dolifque,*
innocuum, fimplex, natum tolerare labores.

But to return to the Bill—the Board of
Commiffioners, as here conftituted, would
have been peculiarly adapted to the objects
for which it was appointed ; the Chan-
cellor of the Exchequer and the Secretary
of State, having officially the moft accu-

rate information, and the moſt extenſive
knowledge of every point of revenue, or
policy, which could be influenced or af-
fected by the tranſactions in India ; the
other Commiſſioners being of his Majeſty's
Privy Council, would probably have been
choſen, as men of eminent abilities, extenſive knowledge, and in ſituations of truſt
and importance in the Government; to this
Board of Commiſſioners, all the diſpatches
received by the Court of Directors of the
Eaſt-India Company, were to be ſubmitted,
" together with all minutes, orders, reſolu-
" tions, and other proceedings of all Ge-
" neral and Special Courts of Proprietors of
" the ſaid Company ;" by theſe means, with
the right of acceſs to all papers and muni-
ments of the Company, which this Bill
was to have given to the Commiſſioners ;
they would have poſſeſſed all the neceſſary,
and indeed, all the poſſible general knowledge of the tranſactions in India, to be
acquired at this diſtance; and have been
fully competent to examine, and decide
upon the expediency and propriety of " all
" letters, orders, and inſtructions whatſo-
" ever,

" ever, relating to the civil government, or
" revenues of the Britifh territorial pof-
" feffions in the Eaft-Indies, propofed to
" be fent or difpatched by the Court of
" Directors of the United Company,"
which were by this Act to have been fub-
mitted to the infpection, and entirely fubject to the decifion, orders, and direction, of
the Board of Commiffioners; thus without
interfering with the minute arrangements
of detail in India, they would have been
able to decide upon all great meafures, and
to prevent the beginning, or ftop the progrefs of any which fhould appear dangerous
to the interefts, or inconvenient to the policy of this country; for the local expediency of any purfuit in India, muft be a fe-
condary confideration, and can no longer be
eligible, when it in any refpect counteracts,
or interferes with the interefts or views of this
country in Europe; therefore the decifions of
the Board of Commiffioners were to have
been conclufive; and, " the faid Court of
" Directors were thereupon to difpatch and
" fend the letters, orders, and inftructions
" fo approved or amended, to their fervants
" in

" in India without further delay, and no
" letters, orders, or inftructions, until *after*
" fuch previous communication thereof to
" the faid Board, were to be at any time
" fent or difpatched by the faid Court of
" Directors to the Eaft-Indies, on any ac-
" count or pretence whatfoever."

By thefe regulations the Government of
the Britifh territorial poffeffions in India,
would have been, as heretofore, carried on by
thofe who beft underftood, and were moft interefted in the management of them; a check
was to have been kept over that Government; and a controul over that management was to be lodged in the hands of
the Minifters of the Crown, to confine
the individual interefts and feparate objects of the Eaft India Company, within the
limits prefcribed by the general policy and
public profperity of the nation at large;
yet, in the midft of thefe neceffary and rigid
regulations for the civil and military government of *territorial poffeffions*, the framer
of the Bill, fcrupuloufly tender of the chartered rights of merchants, cautious of invad-
ing

·ing private property, and aware of the dangerous confequences of fhackling trade, which cannot exift without indulgence, or flourifh under conftraint, had further provided by the act, " that in cafe the faid " board fhould fend any orders or inftruc-" tions, which in the opinion of the faid " Court of Directors relate to points not " connected with the civil or military go-" vernment, and revenues of the faid terri-" tories and poffeffions in India, then, and " in any fuch cafe, it fhall be lawful for " the faid Court of Directors, to apply by " petition to his Majefty in Council, touch-" ing fuch orders and inftructions, and his " Majefty in Council fhall decide, whether " the fame be, or be not connected with " the civil or military government and re-" venues of the faid territories in India, " which decifion fhall be final and con-" clufive." By this regulation the Court of Directors would have had an opportunity of ftating their objections to fuch orders and inftructions, not only before the Board of Commiffioners, but to his Majefty and the remainder of the Council; if it ftill appeared

peared that the orders and inftructions related to objects in the management of which the nation at large were concerned, the decifion was to be conclufive ; and the wifhes and opinions of interefted individuals muft have given way to the purfuit of general advantage.

The appointment of a commander in chief in all or any of the prefidencies or fettlements in the Eaft Indies, to have voice and precedence in the Council immediatley after the Governor or Prefident, was by the act to have been vefted in the Crown ; becaufe the appointment of a General officer from the King's fervice would make him more immediately fubject to the inftructions and directions of the government at home, for the profecution of a war, in which the interefts and profperity of the whole nation muft neceffarily be involved ; and becaufe the co-operation of his Majefty fleets muft be ever better arranged, and more fatisfactory conducted, when the commanders by fea and land act under the fame authority ; and are appointed through the fame channels :

nels : I could urge many more reasons for the
necessity of this single appointment to have
been vested in the Crown by this act, if I
did not apprehend that they might be con-
sidered as invidious ; or, if I did not con-
ceive them to be unnecessary to prove the
expediency and propriety of this regulation :
all other appointments of Governor General, Governors, Presidents, and members of
Councils; in short, to all places of what-
soever nature, degree, or denomination, was
to be left in the hands of the Court of Directors, and Proprietors of East India Stock ;
subject, however, to removal or recall by
order in writing, under the King's Sign
Manual, counterfigned by the Secretary of
State, a copy of the order in such a recall
or removal being transmitted to the Chair-
man or Deputy-Chairman of the Court of
Directors ; who were to nominate and appoint a fit person or persons to supply such
vacancy or vacancies ; to be approved by his
Majesty; or if not approved by him, the
said Court were to proceed to nominate
or appoint some other person or persons,
subject as before to the approbation or difallowance of his Majesty : by leaving the

E   nomination

nomination to all offices with the Court of Directors, the Minifters of the Crown having no fhare in the appointment, and no part of the patronage, could have no inducement from connection to fcreen the mifconduct of delinquents, nor any motive of intereft to tempt them to remove the deferving and diligent fervants of the Company from their offices in India; their attention would probably have been directed to the real merits of the Company's fervants; and the power of removal or recall, have been only exerted for the purpofes of juftice, the prevention of evils, or the punifhment of crimes; the Eaft-India Company would have had confidence in the zeal and abilities of thofe they had themfelves chofen; and the Governors and other officers abroad would be cautious in their conduct, from a knowledge that thofe whofe favour had appointed them to their offices, had not the power of continuing them in their fituations; and that a rapacious acquifition of wealth might excite the envy and clamours of thofe who were no longer poffeffed of the powers, which elfe it might

have

have influenced to protect them; whilft the difallowance given to the Crown of the perfons chofen by the Directors to fucceed to any vacancy, would exclude peculators from an election to any other place, which on any future occafion the influence of their wealth might have fecured to them : Such an equipoife between the divided powers of appointment and removal, would have (as far as human prudence can provide againft human depravity) fecured zeal and moderation in all who had prudence and judgment to fee their real intereft, or at leaft have provided unreftrained and immediate juftice againft thofe who gave way to temptation, or betrayed their truft. As a further barrier againft the operation of any undue influence over the Court of Directors of the Eaft-India Company, and to prevent the delays of chicane and contrivance, at the election of a perfon to fill any office that might become vacant, it was provided by the act, that, if within a ftated period the Court of Directors had not filled up the vacant office, it fhall be lawful for his Majefty to appoint, under his figh manual, a fucceffor to fill

the

the vacaut office. When I confider the whole of this Bill, I am equally aftonifhed at the comprehenfive fyftem of powerful controul, over the conduct of the Eaft-India Company and their fervants, in every point relative to their civil and military government, and in all operations and concerns relative to the *territorial poffeffions* and *revenues* in the Eaft Indies; and at the ftudious forbearance of any affumption of Patronage or influence; the fcrupulous attention to the facrednefs of property, the rigid regard for the commercial rights of a chartered Company, and the noble contempt of illicit power, and unjuftifiable violence, which marks this Bill in contradiftinction to that of Mr. Fox, would have made it an honour to the legiflature had it paffed; it is not for me to decide what conclufion is to be drawn from its rejection.

Having entered fo minutely into the principles and tendency of the two Bills propofed by Mr. Fox and Mr. Pitt, for the regulation of our affairs in India, it will be fcarcely neceffary to draw any other character

ter of either than the nature of their refpective Bills will paint; yet, that no means
in my power may be wanting to awaken my
countrymen to a fenfe of the deep ftake they
have on the event which is to terminate the
prefent arduous political conteft between
thefe two great men, I will endeavour to draw
their characters, according to the opinion I
have formed of each : perfonally a ftranger
to both, having never received any favour
or offence from either of them, I cannot
be fuppofed to be influenced by partiality
or refentment; the diftinguifhing points of
their characters have ftruck me ftrongly; I
fhall defcribe them as I feel them ; and
leave the juftnefs and truth of my delinea-
tion, to be decided upon by the judicious
and difpaffionate obfervers of political tranfactions.

To do juftice to the political character of
a ftatefman, it is neceffary, in fome meafure,
to trace the progrefs of his political life.
No man ever united in himfelf a greater extent of brilliant, dangerous, and powerful
qualities

qualities of the underſtanding than the Right Honourable Gentleman who propoſed the firſt Bill, which I have conſidered in this pamphlet; able, artful, eloquent, judicious, daring, and indefatigable, he began his public life at an early period, with the complicated qualities of an eager voluptuary, and a zealous politician; he united the unremitted enjoyments of a man of pleaſure with the ever preſent proſpect of future greatneſs, and unbounded power; where he could make the two purſuits compatible, he made the firſt ſubſervient to the laſt, and enjoyed their union; where they claſhed he was ſtill mindful that pleaſure was but a tranſient occupation, and that ambition was his great purſuit; he therefore invariably ſacrificed his temporary inclination to his ultimate object. By the disjunction of political connections, and diſunion of family intereſts, he has formed a band of devoted adherents, who are the obſcure attendants of his various tranſitions from precarious power to factitious popularity. Steady to the purſuit of his object; indifferent about the means of its attainment;

unembarraffed by his connections; unreftrained by animofity ; we have feen him at
one time the virulent adverfary, at another,
the pledged affociate of the fame man;
active, ingenious, and clamorous, in oppo-
fition to Government ; enterprifing, inconfiderate, and determined as a Minifter——a
formidable adverfary and refractory col-
league ; he would foon be every thing he
could aim to attain, and more than would
be fafe to the country, if his judgment and
forefight were equal to his quicknefs and
refource ; or that his perfeverance was tem-
pered with prudence, and his enterprize
moderated to probability—the means by
which he laft made his way to power, and
the meafures by which he endeavoured to
preferve it, are glaring inftances of his violent efforts and monftrous refources; having
long ftruggled unfuccefsfully, but ever in-
defatigably, for admiffion to power, he at
length fucceeded in diminifhing the influence of the Crown, which he (not
without reafon) confidered as *one* of the
great obftacles to the attainment of his object, but the diminution of the powers of
Government

Government which enabled him to feize the
direction of it, made him at the fame time
infecure in the poffeffion of his power; to
have reftored the influence of the Crown,
would have been to enfure his immediate
difmiffion, and future exclufion from any
fhare in the Government; fome other
mode was therefore to be adopted for the
affurance of his fituation; the affairs of
India required the interpofition of Government, for their better regulation; his imagination, quick and fertile in expedients,
immediately fuggefted the means of turning
this occurrence to the attainment of his
object, but the impetuofity of his difpo-
fition, and the excefs of his fpirit of enterprize, urged him to attempt the affumption of inaffailable, inftead of confining
himfelf to the poffeffion of well eftablifhed
power; with thefe profpects, and for thefe
purpofes, his Eaft-India Bill was introduced
into the Houfe of Commons—it paffed—
but the Lords, alarmed at the appearance of
a Bill, which fo evidently tended to over-
turn the Conftitution of this Country, without feeming calculated to fettle the Government

vernment of India, rejected it; and his Majesty dismissed Mr. F. from his councils.—The choice of the Crown for a Minister to succeed him, was fixed where the wishes and expectations of the country had also turned; on Mr. Pitt,—a young man of abilities, at least equal in extent to those of Mr. Fox, but very different in their nature—Educated to politics from his infancy, by a father, whose integrity and abilities made him an honour to human nature, and a blessing to his country; the date of Mr. Pitt's political life must be placed at a period long previous to his public appearance, for at his first entrance into Parliament, he burst from the cloud of adolescence, in the full meridian of brilliant eloquence, solid information, and extensive knowledge; proof against the allurements of vice, above the trifling enjoyments of youthful follies, with a spotless character, an unbroken constitution and undivided attention, he devoted himself to the service of his country; his substantial reasoning, and faultless eloquence, pointed him out almost immediately as an object worthy of the most serious attention of all parties : on a change

F
of

of Adminiftration, a place of truft and
confequence was offered to him; fteady,
cool, difpaffionate, and judicious, he determined not to engage himfelf to any
party, till he had tried and proved their
principles; in anfwer to thefe offers, I have
been told, that he declined accepting any
place, declaring that he entertained a good
opinion of the Adminiftration then form-
ing; and, " would watch over them with
" a friendly eye."—At the death of the
late Marquis of Rockingham, a ftruggle
enfued for the firft Poft in Adminiftration;
the unfuccefsful party, without any pretext
of varied meafures, without any pretended
difcovery of altered principles, quitted the
Adminiftration on their difappointment;
fuch a feceffion feemed to forebode the
downfall of the Miniftry; but Mr. Pitt
ftept forth to their fupport, and promifed
to abide by them as long as they adhered to
their principles and conduct; the difad-
vantageous peace, which unavoidably clofed
an unfuccefsful war, occafioned the removal
of that Adminiftration: the hiftory of fub-
fequent ftruggles for power, and the Coalition arrangementsa re foreign to my prefent

fent object, as they are unconnected with the character of Mr. Pitt, till the meafures of that Coalition became the inftrument to fhew him, once more ftepping forward at a moment of difficulty and embarraffment, to fhield the Prerogative of the Crown, the Privileges of the People, and the Conftitution of the Country, from the encroachments of ariftocratic innovations : at firft he ftood alone and unfupported, the *only* champion of the infulted country; but foon his fteady firmnefs fpread its influence to the breafts of others, and he has hitherto been enabled to ftand againft the vigorous efforts of a powerful faction; fupported as he is, by the Corporation of the City of London, and by the body of Merchants, who have been witneffes of the late many ftrange political tranfactions; eminent for the unfluctuating principles of his public conduct, and fcrupuloufly anxious for the true interefts and real profperity of his country, he has foreborne to advife a diffoution of Parliament,—he has offered a Bill, framed, *bona fide*, for the better government of India; unftained by the violation of

F 2 charters,

charters, and feizure of property, unclogged
by glaring innovations on the Conftitution, and a rapacious affumption of unbounded Patronage; yet this Bill has been
rejected by the Houfe of Commons, and leave
has been given for Mr. Fox to bring in another Bill: are then the effential concerns
of the Eaft Indies to be neglected by alter-
nate rejections of different Bills in each Houfe
of Parliament? or is it rather to he wifhed
that Mr. Fox's Bill fhould pafs into a law,
at the expence of the conftitution, and to
the exclufion of every man but himfelf and
his adherents, from the adminiftration of
affairs? The queftion is not now, whether
it is a pleafing or agreeable meafure to dif-
folve the Parliament, but whether it is not
more defirable and more beneficial to the
nation to fuffer *that* inconvenience, than
either to leave the affairs of the Britifh territories in India in confufion, or to fee an
executive ariftocracy independent of the
Crown eftablifhed by act of Parliament,
charters cancelled, and private property fe-
queftered? Why does not the corporation
of the city London, who have addreffed
the

the King, to exprefs their gratitude for
the removal of his Majefty's late minifters
from his Councils, now petition him to
exert his prerogative to fecure their exclufion from them? the ftruggle muft foon
come to a decifion; let the people of England beware of the event; for if it ends in
the removal of the prefent firft minifter, un-
blamed for any error, untried by any meafure, I know not where there will be found
a man to fupply his place, who will poffefs
his candour, integrity, judgment, ability
and moderation; and who will fo juftly poffefs, and fo eminently deferve the confidence of the people of England.

F I N I S.

BEAUTIES of FOX, NORTH and BURKE,

This Day is Published, Price 3s. 6d.

Embellished with a Beautiful Frontispiece of those remarkable Characters, taken from the Life by an eminent Artist:

Together with an ADDRESS to the PUBLIC, and a SERIES of FACTS to the FRIENDS of the COALITION.

Printed for J. STOCKDALE, opposite Burlington-House, Piccadilly.

With a copious INDEX to the whole, in the Course of which, the undermentioned Charges appear exchanged between Lord North, Mr. Fox, and Mr. Burke, and arranged under the following Heads:

Lord NORTH

holds

pronounced

LORD NORTH.

ascribes

Mr. FOX

Mr. BURKE

charges